# POETRY

# &

# MUSINGS

# AN AUTHOR'S
# PRIVATE COLLECTION

# *COPYRIGHT*

Poetry And Musings
An Author's
Private Collection
First Edition
Copyright © Carol Delmornay 2019
All Rights Reserved

. . ❧ . .

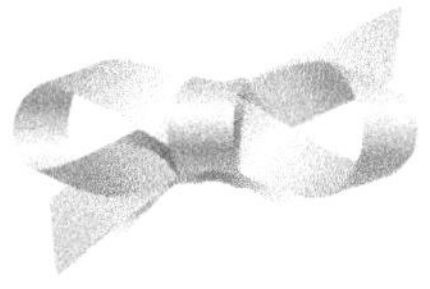

# ASK

Am I asking too much?
For me to receive in return what I freely give
Unyielding in my support
Unwavering in my encouragement
Solid in my praise
Resolute in my devotion
Am I asking too much?
To revel in my excitement
To luxuriate in my passion
To delight in my elation
Am I asking too much?
Evidently ... I am asking too much

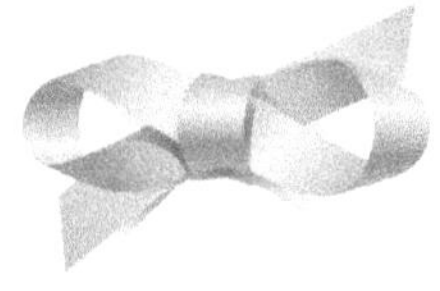

# SURRENDER

Chaos spins through my mind
Whirling my world out of control
Senses reeling with brain in a bind
Brought under control
From the commanding touch
Of Your owning hand
The relief it brings
Makes my heart sing
The calm that descends
Some can't comprehend
such serenity and peace
When I kneel at your feet
Bared and free
Surrendering to you
all that is me

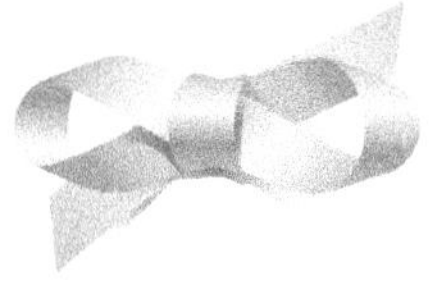

# DO YOU MISS ME?

Do you miss ...
The warmth of my lips
Pressing firmly against your mouth
The way I saturate you
As I tease and seduce with
The rhythm of my tongue
Savoring your taste
The passionate embrace
Of my arms around your neck
As I mold into your shape
Evoking your desire
With every kiss I take
The wanton eager touch
Of my palms upon your chest
Or the stinging of my nails
As they drag along your back
The harshness of my bite
Leaving my mark upon your flesh
My moistened tongue
Gliding along your length
The heat of my mouth
As my lips encompass and descend
Or the tightness of my throat
When I sate my desire to devour
My moans of hunger
Sounds of my need increasing

Or my guttural groans of pleasure
As I hum along your shaft
When I beg you
To stretch me wide
And plunge in deep
To fuck me hard
And fill me with your seed

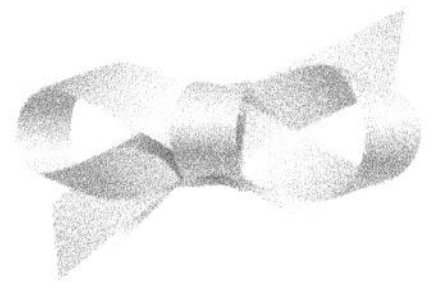

# HEATED GAZE

Gazes meet
Fire ignites
Palms touch
Pure delight
Breaths caress
Hurried and warm
Heartbeats cease
Approaching storm
Lips meet
Feeling heat
Tongues duel
Seductively cruel
Tingling spine
So divine
Lust growing
Juices flowing
Lips swell
Musky smell
Tastes sweet
Such a treat
Fevered flesh
Quivering mess
Hard thrust
Escaping gasp
Sensual moans
Answering groans

Hunger consumes
Desire blooms
Pinnacle reached
Barriers breached
Permission requested
Privilege permitted

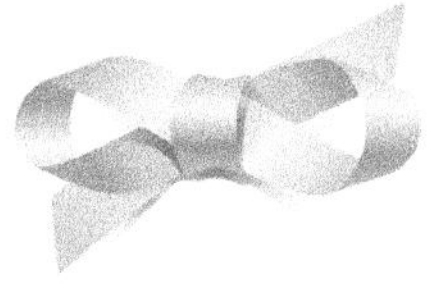

# MISSING YOU

I miss the warmth of your body
Laying by my side
The gentleness of your touch
As your fingers glide
Over the swell of my breast
Across my stiffening peak
A seductive trail
Making my heart beat
Your sudden harsh pinch
That makes me glow
As your fingers travel down
Ever so slow
My heart beat is strong
As you reach my thong
Pushing them aside
Increasing my breath
As one strong finger
Separates swelling flesh
Dipping in the well
Of my climbing desire
The heat of your touch
Driving me wild
I ache for your warmth
And you're loving touch
A feeling I've missed
Ever so much

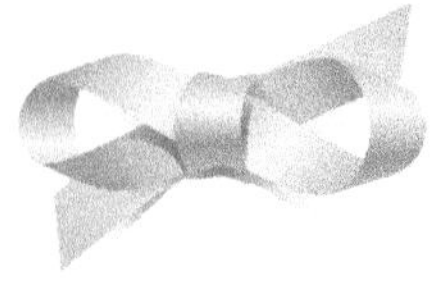

# PATIENTLY

I'll wait ... patiently
To feel your arms wrap around me
To feel your lips encompass mine
To feel your tongue seductively caress
Stirring the embers of desire
As you take away my breath
I'll wait ... patiently
To feel your commanding hands
Arousing my fevered flesh
To feel your fingers teasing and tormenting
Tweaking my stiffened peaks
Enticing lust within to reach fever pitch
I'll wait ... patiently
To feel you tug on my hair
Igniting a burning fire of passion
For your bite to claim possession
And seduce me into submission
To tempt me with your promise
To explore what's dark and forbidden
I'll wait ... patiently
I'll wait as long as it takes.

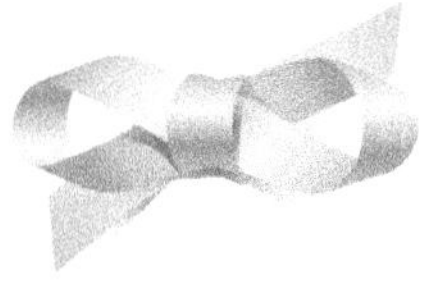

# BETRAYAL

Lonely silence fills the room
Where once laughter and love
Had been in full bloom
Misery and pain
Now fills my heart
Because you're wandering eye
Has ripped us apart
I sit alone in the silence
In front of the hearth
Mesmerized by the flames
Consuming logs in their path
Entranced by the flicker
Of orange and blue
Images of you
Come flooding through
The wind loudly howls
Through the trees
As I recall all the lies
You told to appease
Memories so vivid and clear
My eyes still sting
With unshed tears
Had the ring on your finger
Meant so little to you
That you didn't give a second thought
Of breaking my heart in two

I hope she'd been worth
That long night of desire
The buxom blonde
Who'd set you on fire
You don't think I know
The details of that night
Of the passions that flowed
All through the night
You didn't think
I'd ever find out
But your friends made sure
They sought me out
Their feelings of guilt
Freeing the truth
While I sat all stiff
Silent and mute
Unable to decipher
The tale they told
Your secrets only now
Beginning to unfold
Love is blind
So they say
But did I really have to learn
Of your betrayal
This way
What could have been
Would have been
Should have been
Can now never be
For now it is not "we"
It will only ever be
"Me"

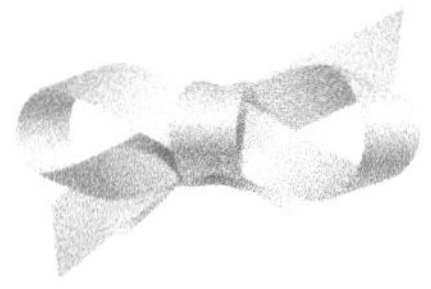

# DESIRE

My desire …
Is to tempt you
to inveigle you to come near
to tantalize and excite
Seduce you to seek out the key
to unlock the hidden temptress
lurking in my depths
Lure you to temerity
to arouse and awaken
the sleeping beast of passion
and succumb to the fiery intensity of lust
My desire …
To satiate my yearning
for permission to worship
to languish in the sanctuary
of the temple that is your soul

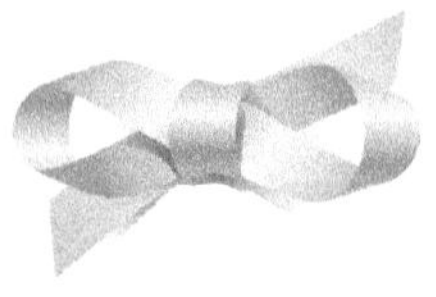

# DREAM

Oceans apart
We've never met
I imagine your breath
On the back of my neck
If I close my eyes ...
I can feel your lips
Brushing ever so gently
Before you nip
Your tongue gliding across
My fevered flesh
The heat of your palm
As you slide and caress
The strength of your fingers
As they pinch and tease
Your hands travel lower
As I beg you ... *please*
My breaths become quicker
As my back arches in
Your fingers slide through
The heat of my cream
You've built my desire
And set me on fire
Enticing my lust
Higher and higher
You're evil grin
Betrays your intent

You're determined to leave me
In utter torment
Opening my eyes
I'm forced to comprehend
My daydream has now
Come to an end

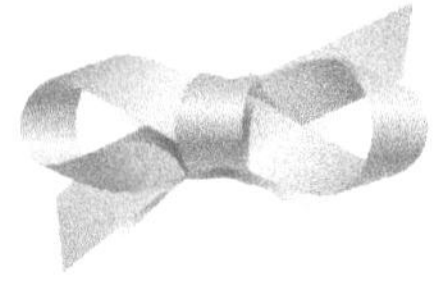

# THE WOLF

The Alpha male waits
Patiently
On the edge of the shadows
Ever present
Ever watchful
Protective of his pack
Guarding all that is his
Powerful
Commanding
Compelling
A natural lordly leader
Confidently playful
A beautifully magnificent creature
The Alpha Male
The Ultra Dominant

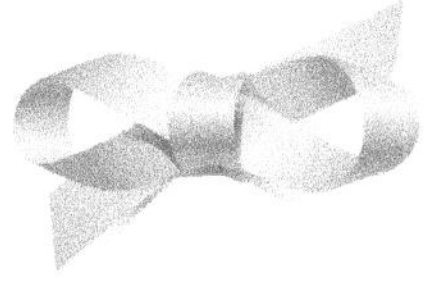

# HEARTBREAK

There are no words
That can accurately reveal
The true sense of loss
That I now feel
My heart is being squeezed
And is about to break
Don't know why I'm surprised
This has always been my fate
I opened myself up
And have only myself to blame
For all this heartache
And emotional pain
Maybe for You
This was all just a game
But I'm here to tell you
This girl did not feel the same
Many tears are there
Just waiting to fall
This girl is determined
Not to curl into a ball
She will rise
Much stronger than before
And rebuild those walls
With single-minded vigor

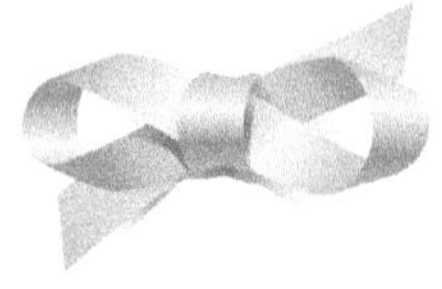

# MISTRESS

Tonight, you're mine
Your hands I will bind
The balance of power
You no longer hold
For tonight is the night
I'm going to be bold
This time *YOU*
Will do as you're told
Let there be no mistake
I plan to tease and titillate
To use my tongue
To bring you undone
Do not be remiss
Remember to call out
"Yes Mistress"

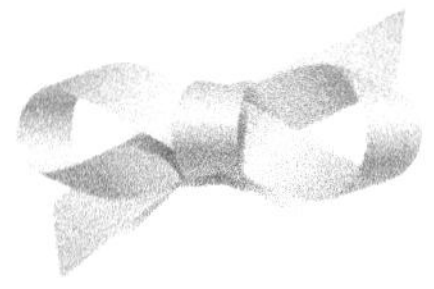

# WANT

I want your firm lips
To dominate mine
Your lascivious tongue
Moist and sublime
To seek through my depths
As you tease and demand
Making me understand
You're in total command
I want your teeth
To clamp down and bite
Pain stirring embers
Within to ignite
I want your strong hands
To bind me in rope
My arms stretching high
As you grab my throat
I want your harsh words
Outlining your intent
Increasing my desire
For sinful events
My body is yours
To do as you wish
Submission to you
My greatest gift

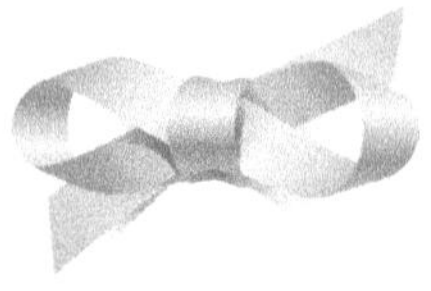

# FATE

Why do I feel compelled to seek you?
Because I am drawn to you
Hypnotically drawn to the dangerous glint
Of fire in your eyes
Captivating, seductive and persuading me closer
Like a moth enchanted with a dancing flame
Tempting me to burn
That steady, unwavering and knowing look
Mesmerising
Stimulating
My heart beats stronger
Faster
Heated blood surging through my veins
Warming and moistening my goosing flesh
Leaving me gasping in a sudden breath
Envisioning the delicious essence of you
Saturating my senses
Craving for a taste
Of the contained control
Emanating from the depths of your soul
One foot in front of the other
My feet took on a mind all of their own
Six-inch stiletto's tapping out a slow beat
Propelling me forward
Insisting I gravitate closer
Unable to resist the magnetic pull

Of your heated gaze
Fixated and holding me a sole captive
In an over-crowded room
The charismatic aura surrounding your frame
Bewitching and scrambling my brain
Driving me insane
My heart beat escalates
Pounding madly inside my chest
My hips swaying with sensuous intent
With every approaching step I take
Distance between us dwindles swiftly
A salacious smirk curling your lips
Portrays the promise of dark desires
That could be mine for the taking
If I dare to take a random chance
Hunger stirs the embers of lust
Excited anticipation fanning the flames
To curl deliciously through my core
Casually leaning your shoulder on the wall
You focus on my advancing form
Your gaze raking slowly down my curves
Pausing with deliberate attention
To appreciate the dips and contours
Of every inch of flesh on display
Leaving the surface of my skin
Tingling with the prospect of your touch
Fulfilling my wildest fantasies
Your hand extends in invitation
As my senses drown in your enticing scent
Your commanding presence intoxicating
Leaving me unable to think
Reaching out my hand

I gasped in a stuttered breath at the electric touch
As palm meets palm
My knees going weak
At the dominating power of your grip
"Do you dare enter the dark side?"
For me, there was no other choice
Than to take that random chance
On a breathless whisper I sealed my fate
"Yes"

# BABY GIRL

A slimming white corset against smooth honeyed skin
Was how I was clothed to begin
Long raven hair tied in one thick braid
Was how he demanded it be every time we played
To wrap it around his unyielding wrist
With strong clenching fingers making a tight fist
His grip unrelenting and firm, swiftly applying pressure
Knowing it'll make me squirm...he was indeed my possessor
Appreciating I'll willingly succumb bending to his every whim
He inserts his thumb with a salacious grin
Through parted lips to play wetly over my tongue
I know pretty soon he'll have me coming undone
Warm breath falls on my neck with his lips near my ear
He whispers deliciously "In here there is no room for fear."
With a black silk blindfold and matching metal cuffs
He takes away my sight and wanton touch
"You are mine to do with as I wish"
His sensual whispered tone had me bewitched
He raised my arms above my head
And tied me securely to the canopy of the bed
The metal cuffs biting in the flesh of my wrist
As his lips sought mine in a deep heated kiss
Savouring my taste with expert precision
He was taming mind and body into submission
Legs suddenly separated, pulled wide apart
Knots in rope done swiftly off by heart

Tethered tightly to bed posts on either side
His husky sensual voice filled with pride
"What a delightful sight you are my baby girl ...
Perhaps I should give the flogger a whirl..."
My breath hitched in on a rapid gasp
As the first stinging swat hit across my ass
Desire burned heatedly from deep within
With every stinging swat on my fevered skin
His finger slides smoothly through my folds
"Oh, baby that is a sight to behold"
Inserting his experienced fingers in my well of desire
Hunger and need spread through me like wildfire
Caressing that sweet spot deep inside, he whispered in my ear
"Do not forget to ask permission, my dear."
With racing heartbeat and panting breath it was too late
Now he would have a punishment to contemplate
Wrists straining against biting black metal
My legs gave in and began to tremble
Unable to utter a request or to simply beg
My body exploded like an ignited powder keg
Ecstasy rolling through in increasing waves
"Oh, baby girl, when will you learn to behave?"

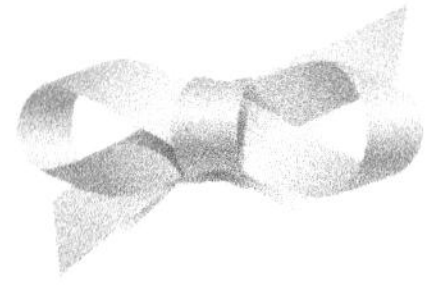

# BELONG

Skin Against skin
I breathe your scent in
Your arms wrapped around
I'm tightly bound
My head on your chest
I'm truly blessed
There's no other place
I feel this safe
Your heartbeat is strong
I'm where I belong

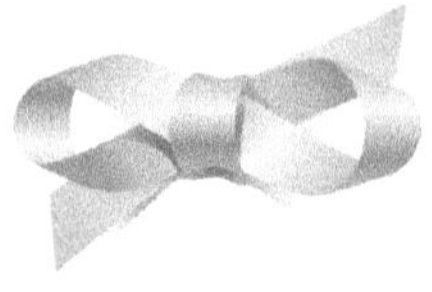

# LETTING GO

You turned my life  
upside down  
was it  
chance?  
fate?  
destiny?  
that dealt me  
that hand?  
You persisted  
until  
I belonged  
to you  
mind  
heart  
soul  
The hardest thing  
I've ever done  
was realizing  
I loved you  
enough  
to let  
you go

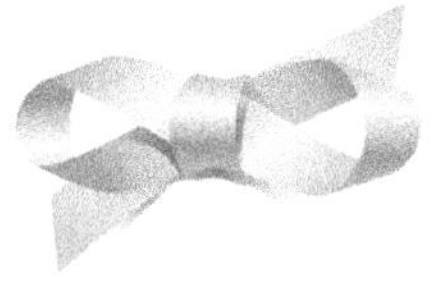

# DELIGHT

I want to melt against
your lean hard body
To luxuriate in the warmth
radiating from you
To blissfully enjoy
your soothing tender strokes
I want to delight
in the strength of you
To drown in the scent
of your unique smell
To revel in the feel of your seductive touch
roaming along my flesh.

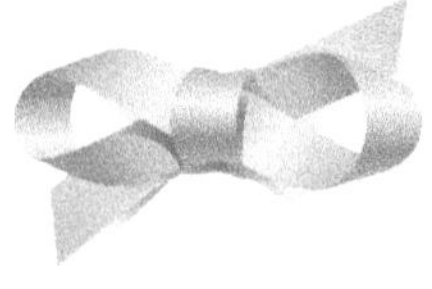

# FOREVERMORE

I fell in love with the soothing
seductive tone of your voice
Your raw masculine sound
connecting deep within me
Calming my restless soul
And I knew long before
I first laid eyes upon you
That I had found
my forevermore

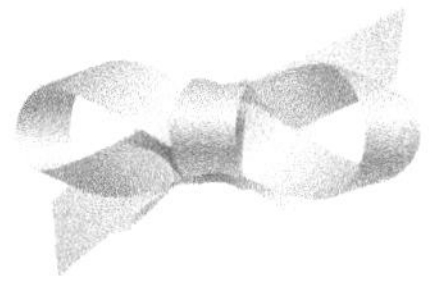

# TREASURE

As the belly grew we began to wonder
Will you be a beautiful little princess
or will you be a handsome little prince
Will your hair be blonde, brown or black,
or perhaps you may be a redhead
Maybe you will have none at all
and be bald
Will you have your mothers
elegant features
Or will you mirror your fathers
ruggedly handsome lines
We are curious to see what you look like,
who you may resemble
As we wait with excited anticipation
for your long-awaited arrival
You decided the day and time
of your entry into this world
We counted ten little fingers
and ten tiny little toes
We were finally able to meet
our handsome little prince
Our hearts were bursting
with a love we never thought possible
Our eyes overflowing with tears
of immense joy
As we stared in wondered awe

at the beautiful little miracle in our arms
From the shock of thick black hair
to the little button nose
And your heart-shaped
rosebud little lips
We know unequivocally
you are our little gift
And we will forever
treasure you

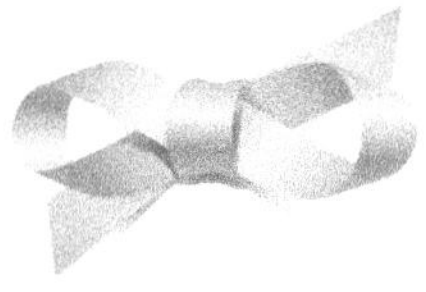

# MASTER'S HAND

His hands are capable of
delivering immense pleasure,
and at times,
insurmountable pain,
they can harshly discipline,
or deliver a teasing touch,
they can gently caress,
or swat a playful sting,
They can teach you, guide you,
control you, calm you,
protect you, possess you,
defend you and love you,
His hands can make you feel cherished,
desired, satisfied
they can build you up...
and they can tear you down...
but trust they will always be there
to catch you when you fall

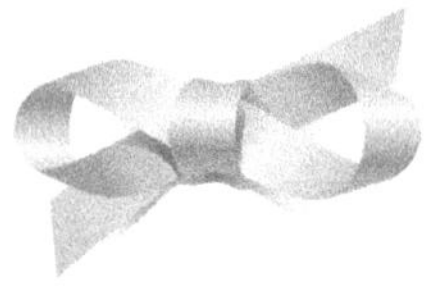

# RUEBEN GEORGE

Sweet little boy
You knew your time was nigh
But you didn't want to go
Without first saying hello
You heard their voices
You felt their touch
Sweet little boy
Mummy and Daddy love you
So, so much
Your wings were sprouting
It was your time to depart
Surrounded in all the love
From your Mother's and Father's hearts
Your time in this world
Was far too brief
And all of our hearts
Are filled with grief
Fly high little angel
Look down from above
Knowing how much
You filled our hearts with love

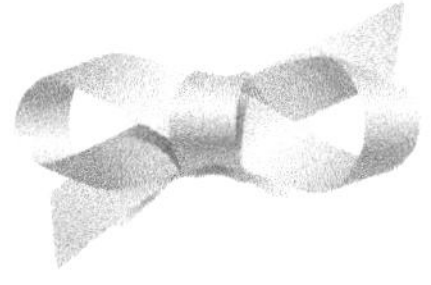

# FIRE

Stoke the fire
of desire
to curl
deliciously
through
every nerve ending
in my body
and bring
every inch
of my skin
to life...

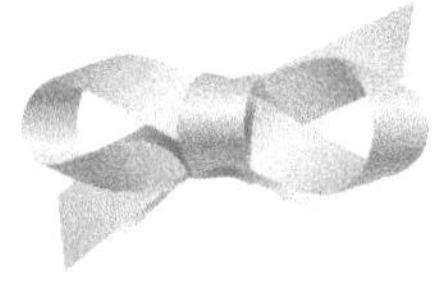

# YEARNING

I want to
explore and touch
your body,
my fingers are yearning
to begin
their maiden voyage,
to discover
the hidden treasures
of your contours.

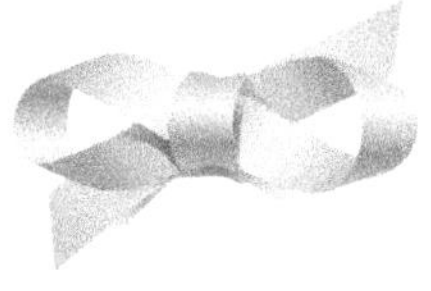

# EROTIC TALE

The most
erotic tale
I'll ever know
is the story
your fingers
imprint upon
my skin

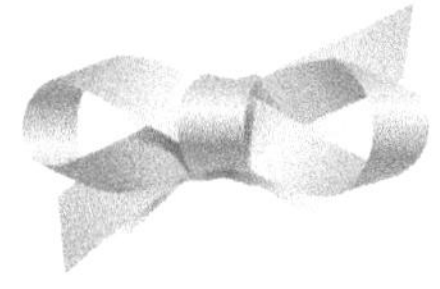

# HUNGER

Make The hunger
Rise inside me
And make
My body quiver
With an awakening
So captivating
My legs
Will weaken
At my knees

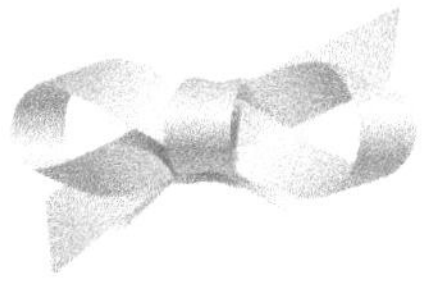

# MASTER'S ENJOYMENT

Do not doubt my enjoyment
At watching the flood of ecstasy
Roll violently through your
Taut muscles ...
To relish
In the lustful moans
And screams of pure bliss
Absently leaving your throat
At the height of
Euphoric release

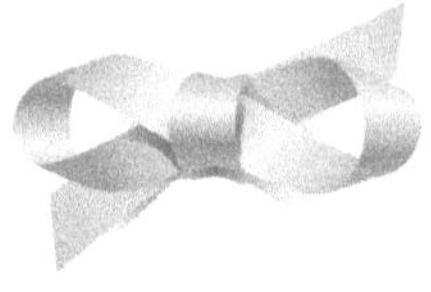

# ABSTRACT MUSINGS

## MASTER'S FLOGGER

Naked, I seductively crawled over into position,
leaning over the seat of the chair at the firm,
but silent direction of one strongly pointed
finger from Master.
My body was warmed from the heat emanating from the
dancing flames of the mesmerizing fire.
The teasing touch of the oiled falls of leather
of Master's flogger whispered enticingly over my heated flesh,
inciting an unhurried wave of goose bumps to wash over me.
All of my attention immediately focused on the climbing
anticipation of feeling the sting that I craved,
the lips of my exposed pussy
slickening at the prospect of them landing
upon the smooth surface of my bared skin.

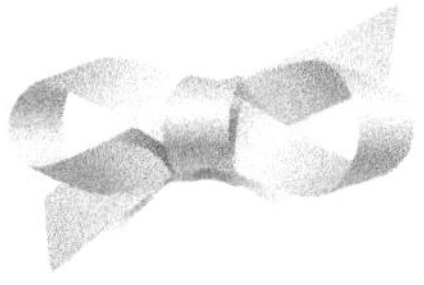

# AN AUTHOR'S PLEDGE

I yearn for my words
to seduce your imagination,
to persuade you to enjoy
a sinful ride of lust,
to feel every line,
and make your heart beat
hard and fast
behind your ribs,
to create a sensual glow upon your skin,
and leave you wet and wanting,
with the desire to hunger for more ...

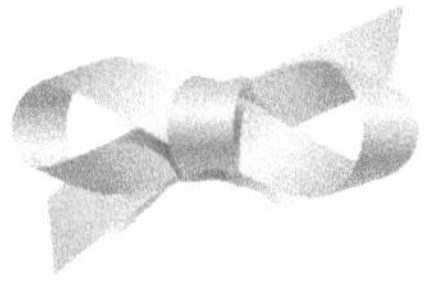

# FOREVER LOVE

Sitting at our favorite place,
smoking a cigarette on the balcony,
I can hear your voice echoing through my mind,
berating me for such a filthy habit,
and telling me one more time to give it up.
I'd ordered my usual dry martini,
and it sat virtually untouched on the top of the small table.
I had on your favorite dress,
the one exposing the dips and contours
of my back that you loved so much.
I could almost feel the heat from your palm as your
finger delicately caressed down the length of
the smoothness of my exposed flesh,
and your hot breath in my ear,
telling me how much you desired my curves,
and the taste of my skin.
A shiver rolled through my body,
and my skin rose up with a million tiny little goose bumps,
waiting for your fevered touch.
If I closed my eyes,
I could feel your lips trailing along my elegant neck,
the moist warmth of your wet tongue sliding up the side,
and the pinch of your teeth as you nipped the bottom
of my lobe while your hand traveled down my back,
and disappeared under the fabric of my dress
to teasingly caress the top curve of my ass

with the tips of your fingers.
I shifted on my seat,
the heat of desire beginning to stir between the
apex of my thighs,
an all too familiar ache growing steadily in my core.
My body craved your touch, your passion;
my ears craved to hear your voice,
and my lips craved for the taste of your skin,
to savor your flavor.
My broken heart swelled with pain.
Why did you have to leave me?
My eyes filled with tears as I looked up at the stars.
I knew you hadn't chosen to leave,
but it didn't ease the pain I felt.
As the first tear rolled down my cheek,
I heard your voice.
"I will love you forever."
I picked up my glass, and raised it to the heavens.
"As I will forever love you…"

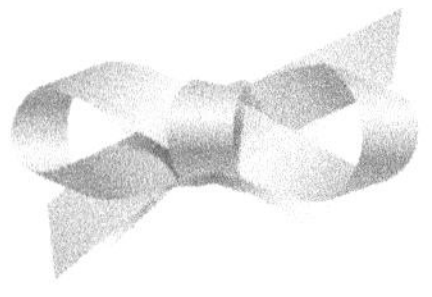

# PROUD

"I'm proud of you."
Just words, but they had a powerful effect on me.
More so than the "I love you," he'd uttered right before them.
Even though we'd had our fair share of ups and downs,
I knew he loved me with every fibre of his being.
He told me he did every single day.
But those words
"I'm proud of you,"
made my heart swell with emotion.
We'd just attended a very sad occasion,
a funeral for a family member.
A funeral also attended by my parents
and an aunt I had not spoken to for 16 years.
Three people I would never speak another word to again.
Some would ask the question how could I not speak to them?
The answer to that was both easy and complex.
I would answer with questions of my own.
Would you speak to them knowing what they had done
to destroy you?
Knowing the lengths they had taken to take your love away?
The constant barbs telling you you would never amount to anything,
that you were a disappointment,
that you were a let-down
because you were was too different?
The black sheep of the family - that's what I'd been labelled.
And they hated the man I had chosen to marry,

the father of my children.
Their hate for him consuming them so much
they had taken the drastic action of trying to take his life
sixteen years ago.
No. I would never say another word to them.
I held my head high.
I was not ashamed of who I was, of who I had become.
I had grown to love myself, to be comfortable in my own skin.
I was confident.
Knowing what I had achieved in my life,
the children I had raised, the love my husband and I shared.
To hear my husband tell me how proud he was of me,
of the way I'd conducted myself,
the charisma surrounding me making me glow,
drawing people to me in spite of the hateful,
evil glares I'd had to endure from three people attending
such a sad occasion,
were words that had a profound effect on me.
I didn't think it was possible to love him any more than I already did.
But he proved it was,
just by telling me he was proud of the woman sitting beside him.
I love you baby...
with everything I am.

# About the Author

Carol Delmornay is a married mother of three young adults, born and raised in the beautiful city of Perth, Western Australia. She and her husband Mark moved to a small town in the Goldfields region of Western Australia in December 2015 to renovate their home and design their gardens. Always a verocious reader, the urge to write didn't hit until later in life. In between attending her children's sporting activities and running a business with her husband, she poured many hours, blood, sweat and tears into her first series---"His Word-The Trusted Saga". Carol also enjoys writing erotic short stories and has written a dark erotic short story that will become a full length novel. She spends all her spare time writing (always has a laptop attached to her hip and about ten works in progress at any one time), and listening to music, swimming, walking, and enjoying the peaceful life the country has to offer.

www.ingramcontent.com/pod-product-compliance
Lightning Source LLC
Chambersburg PA
CBHW071524030726
47593CB00003B/1383